Stepping Over Puddles Of Pain

A Teen's Journey Through Grief

Taylor DuBose

Copyright © 2020 Taylor DuBose
All rights reserved.
ISBN: 978-0-578-67504-6

Book design:
Williams DocuPrep
www.williamsdocuprep.com

Scripture quotations marked KJV are from the Holy Bible, King James Version (Authorized Version). First published in 1611. Quoted from the KJV Classic Reference Bible, Copyright © 1983 by The Zondervan Corporation.

Scripture quotations marked (NLT) are taken from Holy Bible, New Living Translation, copyright © 1996, 2004, 2015 by Tyndale House Foundation. Used by permission of Tyndale House Publishers Inc., Carol Stream, Illinois 60188. All rights reserved.

Taylor DuBose

Contents

Contents 3

Foreword 4

Dedication 9

Acknowledgments 10

Introduction 11

My Dad 14

The Day My Life Changed 23

After the Funeral 32

Understanding Grief 40

Your Support System 52

Let God Help You 63

Scriptures for Comfort 67

Tips to Help You Through the Grief 72

Grief Homework 76

Conclusion 81

Notes 83

Foreward

Apostle Ron Wilson

I have known Taylor all her life. My name is Apostle Ron Wilson. For 33 years, I have served as the Senior Pastor of Full Christian Assemblies International in Hazel Crest, Illinois. I have traveled to five continents and seen families all over the world. The DuBose family has displayed a model Christian family.

The Bible says, "Train up a child in the way he should go: and when he is old, he will not depart from it" (Proverbs 22:6). After the death of her father, Taylor with support from her mother and church family has turned her grief and pain into gain by wanting to help other young people facing the trauma of losing a parent, sibling or other loved one.

I am so proud of Taylor for this great accomplishment and happily recommend this book to people young and old to help walk through their grief journey. My applauds go to her mother, Alice, who has been a perfect role model as a mother guiding her, comforting her, and encouraging her to give back.

Through this book, I hope that you can be encouraged and always remember that it's not always about you, it's about others.

God bless you,
Apostle Ron,
Full Gospel Christian
Assemblies International

* * *

Ann Burns

I knew the day my niece Taylor A. DuBose was born that it was for a great purpose. She's such a purpose-driven teenager. She is driven by God's purposes, not her own. I have seen Taylor overcome great obstacles in her life, like the ones that come to break you down, but Taylor is a fighter.

This book *Stepping Over Puddles Of Pain* will bless many people. The message is to never give up. Keep jumping over the puddles!!!

* * *

Dr. Cynthia Taylor

According to Erikson (1968) adolescence is a period of exploration and vulnerability. It's during this time when young people are exposed to a myriad of potentially life-altering experiences. These life-altering experiences or turning points are considered the focal points of change in one's life. Therefore, how an individual chooses to make meaning, or sense of their turning points is what is essential for positive adjustment.

Taylor, with the assistance of her mother, chose to engage in counseling with me, to adjust to the passing of her dad. The emotions she experienced ranging from sadness, anger, resentment, confusion, frustration, just to name a few, were all a part of her grieving process.

Time, processing, talking, crying, journaling, and giving oneself permission to experience the array of emotions is necessary to heal and get through, not get over, the loss. In working with Taylor, she was able to come to the realization that turning points are specific events that are perceived to alter the normal flow and directions of one's life (Pillemer, 2001).

Grief counseling is a beneficial resource where you learn coping skills, journal your thoughts and feelings, incorporate prayer, reflect, and remember a loved one, all to work through the life-altering experience.

Taylor was open and vulnerable during the counseling process, which helped her to embrace her new normal, and she will continue to do so in the days ahead. Kudos to you, Taylor, for the progress you have made and this book that will help so many young people.

Dedication

This book is dedicated to my dad Todd DuBose. You will forever be in my heart. I thank God for the time we had together, even though it was short. I will love you forever.

Acknowledgments

I would first like to acknowledge and thank God who inspired me to write this book. I would also like to thank my mom, Alice DuBose, who always supports and encourages me.

To my siblings Damaya Knox, Angeleea DuBose, Braylen Bennett, Breyona Bennett your love and support means the world to me. You guys are amazing!

Thank you, Apostle Ron, and Pastor Barbra Wilson, you have been a great support to me since I was born.

Introduction

Hello, my name is Taylor DuBose. This is my story of how I learned to adjust to my dad's passing. I say adjust to because I don't think I will ever get over his passing. I think it just gets easier to deal with as time goes by.

Yes, I am a teenager, but please don't let my young age discourage you. I have learned a lot, changed a lot, and grew a lot since my dad passed. The journey through grief is not the same for everyone, and it can be especially difficult for children and young adults. It has been hard dealing with my father's passing. What helped me most was prayer and drawing closer to God.

As I prayed through my journey, I prayed for other young people who have lost a parent, sibling, or other loved one. This helped me take the focus off me. It was God who encouraged me to write a book on grief from a teen perspective. In this book, I share how I learned to deal with my dad's passing and move forward.

Although I wrote this book for young people, the information and tips I share can help every person, young and old move forward through this difficult time to their new normal.

Here is my story . . .

My Dad

My dad, Todd DuBose, was a friendly and kind man who treated people well all the time. He was the type of person who never met a stranger. Dad knew everybody on earth, so I know all the angels already knew him when he got to heaven.

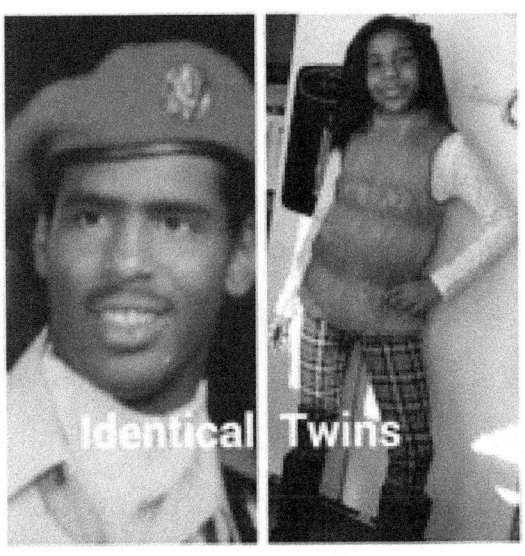

Identical Twins

His family was the most important thing in life to him.

He was six-foot three-inches tall, and very handsome. People say I look just like him. We look so much alike that people would say to him, "That child is your twin. She looks just like you."

He would often joke and say, "Daddy's baby, Mama's maybe. If your mom takes me to court, she'll be kicked out because we look just alike."

He always made me feel special. Even the littlest things he did would make me happy. For instance, when he would get off work, he would drive his truck in the garage and blow the horn and not stop until I ran out the door.

When I heard his horn, I knew it was time to go to our favorite place—7-Eleven, to get our nightly slushes. Dad always got the Big Gulp slush. I could put any flavor I wanted in mine. He knew that I loved Butterfinger candy bars, so sometimes he would bring me one when he came home.

Dad loved to play his music loud when he was driving. He always played his favorite song *There Goes My Baby* by Charlie Wilson. He would let the windows down, and I would let my hair fly in the wind. I thought I was in heaven.

Other times, we would go to Dollar Tree, and he would say, "Taylor Bug, you've got five minutes to pick out any toy you want." He would count to five and I would quickly run off to find the toy that I wanted.

Dad loved sports and celebrating the holidays. Christmas, the Fourth of July, and Memorial Day were his favorites. He was a great cook on the grill. Every 4th of July he would buy a lot of food and invite every person he knew to come to over, so he could show off his grilling skills.

He especially loved Christmas. He would wake us up at five in the morning to open our presents. He loved seeing us happy and he would take a lot of pictures.

Dad always made me feel special. He supported me in everything I did. One Sunday while I was singing Tasha Cobbs

Leonard's *Break Every Chain* in church, Dad was so excited for me that he could not sit down. Before I could finish the song, he ran on to the stage, picked me up in his arms, spun me around, and with tears running down his face, he said, "That's my baby."

I laughed and whispered, "Dad everyone knows that I'm your daughter."

My dad was my hero and my best friend. He always made me feel safe. I didn't worry about anything when he was around because he was my protector. Even though he is with God now, I still think of him as my protector. I know that both he and God are looking down from heaven at me, shielding and protecting me.

Dad always made sure that our vacations were special. One of my favorite places to go was Wisconsin Dells. It was so funny to see him act like a kid in a candy store when we went there. Dad and I would stay in the water all day. We would have so much fun. We would talk, play, and sing together. Sometimes my friends could come along, and that was a lot of fun too.

Dad always encouraged me to do my best and make good grades. He supported me in everything I did. He came to every event I had at school, church, or any activity. He believed in me and helped me believe in myself.

The last Sweetheart Dance we attended we dressed alike. I wore a beautiful cream, gold, and black dress. Dad wore a black suit with a cream shirt. We looked good! We danced to Charlie Wilson's *There Goes My Baby*. That night is one of the best memories I have of my dad.

When I wanted to become a cheerleader dad encouraged me to do it. He came to all my competitions. He was the loudest person in the building. The last one he attended lasted for eight hours, but he did not care because I was performing. I had no idea that this would be our last outing together.

There was nothing that my Dad would not do for his baby girl. My wish was his command. People said he was wrapped around my finger. I don't know about that, but for me, it was like time stood still when we were together. Then, one day, my world came tumbling down.

The Day My Life Changed

The day my life changed was Wednesday, March 28th, 2015. It started out as a normal day. It had snowed, and it was very cold outside. My dad had cooked dinner and was downstairs in the den relaxing, watching the basketball game.

Then it happened...

In my mother's words, he called her on the phone, and she could barely hear him. Since he was always joking around, she thought he was playing a joke on her. He hung up and called her again. Then, she knew something was terribly wrong. He whispered, "Help me."

Mom took out running downstairs. He wasn't in the family room. She ran through the garage and into the basement. Her heart dropped, she said when she saw Dad lying on the floor. His speech was slurred. She immediately called 911. My cousin Sheila, who is a nurse, was visiting from Arkansas. She worked with dad until the paramedics got there.

My Dad was such a selfless person that

he told my cousin, "I am sorry you came all the way from Arkansas, and here I am sick."

She said, "Uncle Todd, you are going to be okay."

However, it went downhill from there. I later learned that Dad had suffered a massive stroke. When the paramedics got to the house, my aunt sent me to my room while they worked on my dad. I was scared and snuck back downstairs. When I saw my dad lying on a stretcher, I was more afraid. I had no idea that when they took him to the hospital, I would never see him alive again!

Dad had been in the hospital for a couple of days, when I asked my mom if I could go to the hospital and see him. She said he was in the Intensive Care Unit (ICU) and children were not allowed. I later learned that he was in a coma and on life support.

Then, Dad took a turn for the worse and the doctors had him flown to Rush Hospital, a top hospital in Chicago. He had died before he made it there. The doctor called and told my mom he did not make it.

When I heard the news of his death, it was like somebody had punched me hard in the stomach. I screamed in shock and began to cry uncontrollably. I kept thinking, *"He's dead! My dad is dead! This cannot be real!"*

When we got to the hospital, the doctor

and nurses were crying. My mom let me go into the room to say my final goodbye to dad. I called out to him, but he didn't wake up. I just wanted him to wake up and talk to me, but it didn't happen. None of this seemed real!

When we got home, I asked my mom and my aunt what happens when people die. They said people go to heaven to live with God. They told me we would have a funeral service to celebrate my dad's life. My mom said our family and his friends would come to say their goodbyes, pay their respects, and support the family. I asked mom could I sing a song during the service.

She asked, "Can you really do it, Taylor?"

"Yes, I can do it," I said.

Mom and dad loved to hear me sing and I wanted to do this for my dad. I knew I would be singing for him in heaven, so I chose Whitney Houston's song, *I Will Always Love You.*

Then came the day I dreaded—my dad's funeral. I had never been to a funeral, so I wasn't sure what to expect. I had so many emotions running through me I had trouble sleeping the night before. I feared attending my dad's funeral and singing the song to him without crying.

When I woke up that morning, I was exhausted because I hadn't slept. As I was getting dressed for the service my heart felt like it would beat right out of my chest.

The limousine arrived and the funeral people gathered everyone together and led us to the cars. As I stood in front of my house I thought, *"Well, this is it."*

While we were riding in the limo, headed to the church for the funeral service, I was trying to be strong for my family. My aunt must have seen me struggling because she told me it's better to cry and let it all out.

I couldn't let it all out. I needed to be strong so I could sing for my dad. Besides, I felt crying in front of people showed weakness.

When we arrived at the church, people kept wanting to hug me, but I didn't want to hug anyone. I just wanted all this to be over.

The funeral service was sad. It felt like the longest time of my life. Mom was crying, my aunts, and sisters were crying. I was full of anxiety, but I was trying to be strong so I could get through the song for Dad.

I was sad when I went up to sing, but even with all the sadness in my heart I sang it well. I know Dad was smiling at me from above and telling the angels how well I can sing.

As I walked out of the funeral service with my family following the casket, I couldn't hold back the tears any longer. I decided that I did not want to go to the gravesite for the burial. I told mom, "You've got it from here." I sat in the car during that part of the service.

After the Funeral

Back at home, our house was full of family, friends and lots of food. I didn't want to be around anyone, so as soon as I could, I went to my room to lie down.

As I lay there, I cried so hard I thought I might break. I couldn't believe it. I had lost my best friend, my biggest support, and my biggest fan. My dad was dead! I could not imagine living without my dad. I cried until I drifted off to sleep. I woke up the next day feeling the same.

For weeks, my emotions were all over the place. I was angry, hurt, sad, and disappointed. I was mad at God. I knew that He is the one who decides how long we live, and when we die. I felt that He had taken my father away from me, and I was mad. I continually asked God questions like, "Why did You have to take my dad? Why couldn't he watch me grow up? Who's going to take me to the Sweetheart Dance now, God?"

The grief was so heavy that some days I could barely move. I cried all day and all night! I hated going to school. I hated going to church. I did not want to attend family gatherings. I wouldn't sleep for days at a time. Everywhere I looked, everything I did reminded me of my father. I stayed to myself because I did not want people to see me crying. I didn't want to appear weak.

People would say things to me like, "Your dad is in a better place. He's home with the Lord." I know they were trying to make me feel better, but they didn't. I felt the best place for my dad, was to be with me. My whole life would be different if he were still here. I did need help, but those words did not speak to any of the thoughts I was having, or answer any of my questions.

I wondered who would take care of me if I lost my mom, my aunts, or my uncles.

These are the thoughts that ran through my mind, and still do.

The grief was so overwhelming that it was making me sick. One day during class, I was crying so hard that I got lightheaded and passed out. My mom and the paramedics were called. When my mom got there, I was awake, but it was decided that I go to the emergency room (ER).

My mom wanted to ride in the ambulance with me, but the paramedics suggested she follow in her car. The school secretary said she would ride with me. I was nervous and afraid, so she held my hand, which calmed me down. At the hospital, the doctors checked me out and ran some tests. All the tests came back normal. The doctor said I was under too much stress.

The people at my school were so awesome. The principal, teachers, parents, and students called to check on me. They really made me feel loved, but the grief was still very heavy. My mom tried to help, but nothing soothed my soul.

I thank God for a mom who loves me so much. She saw I was in trouble and would not let me stay in that dark place. She took me from doctor to doctor, but they couldn't find anything physically wrong with me. She didn't stop there. She kept searching for something to make me better. What I had was a broken heart, and we did not know how to fix it.

Mom spent hours searching for a good therapist. Finally, she found Dr. Cynthia Taylor, the best therapist money could buy. This was the best decision mom could've made for me. Talking with the therapist helped me open up about my pain and learn to deal with my feelings.

Dr. Taylor gave me the tools I needed to cope with the grief. I learned that grief is a process and that it is not a quick fix. I also learned that everyone's grief is different and not to let anyone put a time limit on it.

It took a long time for me to accept that my dad was actually gone. For the longest time, his death didn't seem real. It still feels unreal sometimes. When someone we love passes, our entire life changes. I enjoyed school and spending time with my friends, but after my dad passed, I found it hard to focus.

I distanced myself from my friends. I went from being a straight-A student to making C's. I stopped talking to my friends. I felt like we didn't have much in common anymore. I believed that no one would understand what I was going through. I just wanted to isolate myself from the world.

When I hear my friends whine and complain about their parents, it upsets me. It's all I can do, not to scream out loud. I say to them, "You do not know how quickly life can change. You should appreciate that your parents are still here, even if you don't agree with what they do or say. I wish I could hear my dad fuss at me again. I wish I could take back the times when I got mad because he would not let me do something that I wanted to do."

They usually get silent and say, "Yeah, I guess you're right," and quickly change the subject.

Understanding Grief

Grief is deep sorrow brought on by someone's death or other loss. Grieving is the natural reaction to loss, especially the loss of someone that we loved who has died. Losing someone you love is painful.

Grief can be confusing and overwhelming. It has been my experience that grief affects you emotionally, socially, physically, mentally, and spiritually. It is different for everyone. It takes on different shapes, attitudes, and behaviors.

Teens may experience grief differently than adults. We may find it harder to express our feelings and accept help. Boys might be under the impression that it's not cool or manly to show emotion or cry. Many teens are afraid that their friends will mock them for showing emotion.

Some emotions of grief can be easily shared with others, and some may be difficult to put into words. The way grief is experienced and expressed is different from person to person. One person may need to talk a great deal about the loss and the pain, and another may become quiet and withdrawn. Some try to avoid facing their pain by holding feelings inside and acting as though they are fine.

Although it is painful and difficult, expressing your grief is important. At times, it might seem like your life is out of control. It is difficult to control the emotions, thoughts, or physical feelings associated with a death.

Watching my family after my dad died, I could see that people grieve differently. Some common reactions of grief include:

- Crying. Crying is healthy. It is not childish or a sign of weakness.

- Stomachache or nausea.

- Heaviness in the chest or tightness in the throat.

- Trouble sleeping or troubling dreams.

- Loss of appetite or increased appetite

- Not wanting to talk.

- Distracting yourself from your own feelings by taking care of everyone else.

- Feeling like you have no energy.

I learned that dealing with death does not follow any rules. There is no right or wrong way to grieve. Sadness and crying may be one person's way of grieving. Laughter and humor could be another person's response.

The way a person grieves can also depend on the personality of that person and the relationship they had with the deceased. For instance, a wife's grief over losing her husband will be different from a child's grief of losing a father, even though they are the same person.

How a person handles grief can depend on their religious and cultural background, and support systems. It can also depend on:

- Circumstances of the death (how, where and when the person died).

- If the nature of the relationship with the deceased was abusive or conflictual.

- If the person found the body of the deceased.

- If the griever was involved in the dying process. Did they have a chance to say goodbye?

- The emotional and developmental age

of the teen.

- The person's previous experiences with death.

Like with me, your relationship with your friends may change. People just don't know what to say to us when someone dies. So, they don't invite you to events, and they don't come around like they used to. You may begin to withdraw from your friends and even your family.

Remember when I said that I felt different from my friends now? If your relationship with your friends has changed, don't beat yourself up about it. You are different now. If they are really your friend, in time things will work out.

If you feel like I feel when I hear people

complain about their parents or siblings. I encourage you to speak up, in a loving way, when they complain about them. It may make them appreciate their family more.

Stages of Grief

Your grief experience will be unique, yet it may include some of the same stages or emotions others experience which may include:

- **Shock and Denial:** This is usually the first response. At least it was for me and others I've talked to. You just shake your head and say, "No. This can't be happening."

- **Pain:** Once the shock decreases you begin to realize that the person is really gone, and it can be difficult to handle. I tried to hide what I was feeling, but it only made me sadder and more depressed. Take it from me, it is important not to hide your pain just so you can be strong for others.

Some teens try to avoid or escape the pain by acting out, drinking, or using drugs, or they may develop eating disorders. Please do not start down that path. If you find yourself unable to cope, please speak with your parents, your school counselor or someone you trust.

- **Guilt and regret**: These are natural thoughts and feelings when dealing with grief. You may regret something you did or said or didn't say to the person who died. Although it is normal to have regrets or feel guilty, you must remember no one is perfect. Everyone makes mistakes, so don't feel bad or guilty about what you didn't do or say.

Some teens feel guilty because they couldn't stop the person from dying. Remember, it is God who decides how long we live. Everyone dies. When God says it is time to die no one can stop it. You could not have prevented it, even if you tried. The reality is that you have no logical reason to feel guilty. Forgive the person and forgive yourself.

Some people even feel guilty about wanting to move on, fearing they will forget their loved one. I don't believe your loved one wants you in pain. I believe they want you to move on and live. You will never forget them. Cherish the memories and the love you shared with them. Live and do good. Think of them as watching over you, cheering you on.

- **Anger and Depression:** You may begin to lash out at others because of all those emotions you are experiencing. Please remember just because you are hurting, does not mean it's okay to be mean to others.

  You may also withdraw from people and become extremely sad and cry often. You might notice changes in your appetite or sleep patterns.

- **Acceptance and Hope:** Eventually you will come to accept the loss. You begin to adjust to life without the deceased.

Seek Help If You Need It

Losing a parent, sibling, friend is tough. It's okay to seek help if you need it. Dr. Taylor helped me tremendously. Here are some signs that you may need to seek some outside help to process your grief.

- Isolation from friends and family.
- Changes in behavior or appearance.
- Changes in sleeping or eating patterns.
- Lack of motivation, skipping school, or dropping grades.
- Overwhelming social, family, or academic pressure.
- Depression or unusual levels of anxiety.

- Talk of suicide or a fixation on death.
- Constant feelings of anger or guilt.
- Reckless sexual behavior.
- Drug use.

If you think you need help, talk to your parents, school counselor, pastor, or someone you trust and let them help you find help.

Your Support System

I thank God for my mom, who even though she was grieving herself, noticed that I was having a very hard time dealing with the passing of my father. I didn't want to be a burden to my family. They were going through enough, and I didn't want to make their grief more difficult.

Besides, I really thought that people

noticed my sadness, and would just run to my rescue. I didn't know I might need to reach out, or not withdraw when they tried to help. I was so busy trying to be strong that I didn't realize that I wasn't being strong at all. I didn't realize that I had a wonderful support system in place, people who were ready to help me if I asked.

You may think people should just know that you are having a hard time and come to your rescue. However, if you push people away, how can they help you? And if you never let on that you need help how will they know?

Your family and friends may think your silence means you are okay. You should also remember they have their own lives and their own problems going on. More than likely, they want to help, you just need to let them know you need help.

My mom and my therapist encouraged me to open up and reach out to those around me and let them help me through. Once I did, I realized that I had a wonderful support system.

My Uncle Tony is the best uncle that ever lived. When my dad passed, Uncle Tony stepped right in as a father figure. He moved from Arkansas to Illinois to be with me and my sister.

He took me to school every day, and he

made sure I was never late. After school, we would stop and get something to eat. Uncle Tony took me anywhere I needed to go. I named the city; he said let's go. Still, years later, he's still with me, going through a hard time. I can always count on him, and I owe him my life.

Look at the people around you. I'm sure you have someone in your corner like my Uncle Tony. They may not move to another state, but they are there when you need them to help you make it through the day. Please remember you are not a burden because you need help.

My Auntie Anne is like my second mom. She's a great teacher and listener. I can talk with her about anything and tell her my deepest secrets and not worry about her telling anyone.

My little Sister Damaya is also a great part of my support system. She always has my back and I have hers. My Auntie Vera Washington is another great support. Many times, when I thought I couldn't make it, she would build me back up.

Auntie Angie is my rock. She loves me unconditionally and has always supported me. When I visit Tennessee on vacation, she will drive an hour to come and cook me some chicken alfredo. She makes the best!

Then there is Uncle Mark, my dad's brother. He is kind, like my dad. He always calls me and says, "Taylor, I'm always here for you any time." I love talking with him.

His voice is so soothing, it makes me feel like my father is talking to me.

My Pastors Apostle Ron and Pastor Barbara Wilson are a great part of my support system. They are the type of pastors that people dream of. I know that I can call them any time, and they will be there. They always encourage me to trust and lean on God. Apostle Ron treats me like I am his granddaughter. If you belong to a good church, your Pastor and the other ministers are a good source of support to help you walk through this difficult time.

My Aunt Sheila would drive eight hours back and forth to check on me. When she couldn't make the drive, she would call and check on me. Uncle Robert, my cool uncle believes in me and makes me believe I can do anything. He is an anchor to me.

My Aunt Mary Burns and Auntie Debbie Reeves who recently passed away were always there for me. Aunt Mary Burns constantly assured me that I can do whatever I set my mind to. Auntie Debbie was a rock when I need one. I miss both of them dearly. My Uncle Sidney Moore is an awesome uncle! He comes to visit every day and takes me wherever I need to go.

My Godmother Joette Ogburn is my prayer warrior. She has had my back ever since I was born. My grandparents are deceased, but Ella Samuels, my spiritual grandmother, steps in doing the things that grandmothers do. She is amazing.

My Uncle Allen Weaver, my dad's best friend, is there for me too. My friends Jeremiah, Tru, Jaylin, Romania, Takiya, and Destiny are very supportive friends. They are shoulders that I lean on when I am feeling low.

Heilga Rankins is so loving and compassionate towards. She has no children of her own and treats me and my sister as if we are her children.

Apostle Greg and Pastor Tina Jacobs were my dad's good friends who are always there for me and my sister to make sure that we are fine.

These are some of the people who are an important part of my support system. There are many more, too many to name them all. This awesome group of people are there for me cheering me on in life. I don't think I would be as far along as I am, or able to write this book had it not been for them.

The grief journey can be long and hard. If you try to do it alone, it will be much harder, and much longer. Whether you are dealing with grief or just everyday life, you need a good support system around you. However, in a time of grief, a good support system is very important.

Recognize Your Support System

Who are the people who were there for you before your loved one passed? Who did you turn to when you needed advice?

Recognize, these are the people who will help you deal with the pain.

Some examples of people who could be your support system might include your parents, siblings, grandparents, and other family members. Your close friends, teachers, school counselors, and pastors can also be a part of your support system.

Chances are, there are many people around you who would like to be there to help you. Make a list of the people you believe you can depend on to help you ease your burden and grief. Call on these people when you need someone to cry to, someone to laugh with, or when you feel weak or need something.

Don't be afraid to ask when you need

something. These people care about you and call on them when you need someone. Don't forget to pray and call on God, He is always ready to listen and help you in your time of pain.

Let God Help You

After the funeral, your family and friends will eventually return to their busy lives, but your grief will still be very real. God is never too busy. He will always be there to help you.

Once I began to work through my anger, I realized that God was actually working behind the scenes, helping me in several ways. He used my family and my support system, my therapist, prayer, my pastors, church family and His Word to bring me through to where I am today. I believe that He will be with me every day of my life.

I encourage you to hold on to God and let Him help you through this hard time. Isaiah 40:29 says, "He gives power to the weak, and to those who have no might He increases strength." (NKJV)

My relationship with God has grown. I talk to Him every day. I read my Bible more. I don't know what your relationship is with the Lord, but I encourage you to let Him help you get through the grief.

Knowing that the Lord loves me, gives me peace. The more I get to know God, the more I learn that there is nothing our God cannot do. He can heal the pain and hurt your heart is going through.

How do you get to know God? First, you must believe that He exists. Then, you must believe that He sent His Son Jesus to the Cross to die for your sin. You must believe that Jesus died on the Cross and rose from dead, so we could be connected back to God by faith.

"For God so loved the world that He gave His only begotten Son, that whoever believes in Him should not perish but have everlasting life. For God did not send His Son into the world to condemn the world, but that the world through Him might be saved."- John 3:16-17 NKJV

"...that if you confess with your mouth

the Lord Jesus and believe in your heart that God has raised Him from the dead, you will be saved. For with the heart one believes unto righteousness, and with the mouth confession is made unto salvation."
– Romans 10:9-10 NKJV

The Bible says believing on Jesus is the way to God. If you have not accepted Jesus Christ as Savior, I encourage you to search your heart and make that choice.

Then, grow your relationship with God by praying, spending time in His Word, and attending a good church so you can learn more about Him. No matter how young or old you are, your relationship with God is the most important relationship you can have.

Scriptures for Comfort

The Bible is full of promises from God, that He will be there and take care of us in good and bad times. His word gives me assurance that everything will be okay.

Here are some scriptures that you can meditate on (think deeply or focus on) when you are feeling sad.

- **Matthew 5:4** *"God blesses those who mourn, for they will be comforted."* (NLT)

You may not feel blessed right now, but you are! This verse says that *"you shall be comforted."* Take all those feelings to God and talk to Him about them.

- **Matthew 11:28** *"Come to me, all of you who are weary and carry heavy burdens, and I will give you rest." (NLT)*

Grief can make you feel like a ton of bricks are on you. I encourage you to let God help you.

- **Psalm 34:18** *"The Lord is close to the brokenhearted; he rescues those whose spirits are crushed." (NLT)*

God can keep you from being consumed by it, but you have to admit you need help. You must ask God to help you.

- **1 John 5:14** *"And we are confident that he hears us whenever we ask for anything that pleases him." (NLT)*

  This scripture says we can trust that God hears us when we pray according to His will. His will is for you to be at peace and comforted. When we are feeling bad, God's will is for us to come to Him so He can help us get past it.

- **Psalm 23:4** *"Even when I walk through the darkest valley, I will not be afraid, for you are close beside me. Your rod and your staff protect and comfort me." (NLT)*

- **Romans 8:28** *"And we know that God causes everything to work together for the good of those who love God and are* *called according to his purpose for them." (NLT)*

- **1 Peter 5:7** *"Casting all your anxiety on Him, because He cares for you."*

- **Isaiah 49:13** *". . . For the Lord has comforted his people and will have compassion on them in their suffering." (NLT)*

- **Isaiah 41:10** *"Don't be afraid, for I am with you. Don't be discouraged, for I am your God. I will strengthen you and help you. I will hold you up with my victorious right hand."*

- **Romans 8:38** *"And I am convinced that nothing can ever separate us from God's love. Neither death nor life, neither angels nor demons, neither our* *fears for today nor our worries about tomorrow—not even the powers of hell can separate us from God's love."* (NLT)

- **2 Corinthians 1 :3-4** *"Blessed be God, even the Father of our Lord Jesus Christ, the Father of mercies, and the God of all comfort; Who comforteth us in all our tribulation, that we may be able to comfort them which are in any trouble, by the comfort wherewith we ourselves are comforted of God.." (ESV)*

Tips to Help You Through the Grief

Moving on after the death of a loved one can seem like you are forgetting the person, but this is not true. The person was a part of your life. No one can replace them, and you will never forget them. Moving on only means accepting what has happened.

Here are some things that helped me move forward. I believe they will help you move on with your life too.

Talk It Out

In the beginning, it was difficult to talk about my feelings; but once I did, it helped me. You cannot do this alone. You need someone to confide in. Someone who will listen as you acknowledge your pain. I talked with Dr. Taylor and family members that I trusted. Call on a trusted family member or friend, school counselor or pastor.

Start a Journal

Keeping a journal or a notebook and

writing about your experience and what you are feeling will help you come to grips with what is happening. You can share things that you find hard to share out loud.

Write A Letter to the Deceased

Write a letter to the person who died. Tell them how you feel, what makes you angry or sad, all the things you meant to say, or need to say. It will make you feel better.

Create a Special Keepsake

Start a memory book, make a memory box, or video. Include special pictures and thoughts and wonderful memories that you want to cherish. As times goes by, you can refer to it often. It will make you smile.

Take Care of Yourself Physically

People say that exercise relieves stress, anger, and sad emotions. Eat healthy foods and snacks. A healthy diet will keep your physical body in good health and promote a better wellbeing.

Join A Support Group

If you don't have a trusted friend who will listen, then join a support group. Being with other teens who have experienced a loss is comforting. It will give you a safe place to share your thoughts and express your what you are feeling.

Grief Homework

Take some time and answer the following questions. They will help you work through your grief. You may need extra paper for some of these.

1. What is something that you're good at to clear your mind of other thoughts crowding in on you?

   _____

   _____

_____

_____

_____

_____

_____

_____

_____

2. List some of the ways your loved one touched you, influenced you, gave to you, loved you.

_____

_____

_____

_____

3. The deceased person played a big role in who you are today. How can you give thanks in their memory and share the love they shared with others?

_____

_____

_____

_____

_____

_____

4. Write a letter to someone you know who has lost a loved one. Use your own pain to show compassion for them.

_____

_____

_____

_____

_____

_____

5. What do you want your life to look like in six months?

Conclusion

I have finally gotten to a happy place. You will get here too.

Please take one day at a time. The pain will get easier and soon dissolve.

Don't try to put a time limit on the

grief. Call on God. He is a present help in times of trouble (Psalm 46:1). Talk to Him often. If you do not know Jesus; if you don't have a relationship with Him, get to know Him. The joy of the Lord will be your strength (Nehemiah 8:10).

The Bible says in Psalm 30:5, *"weeping endures for a night, but joy comes in the morning."*

The morning will come!!!!

Taylor

Notes

Stepping Over Puddles Of Pain

Taylor DuBose

Stepping Over Puddles Of Pain

www.ingramcontent.com/pod-product-compliance
Lightning Source LLC
Chambersburg PA
CBHW071412290426
44108CB00014B/1786